HAL LEONARD *Even More* EASY POP BASS LINES

BASS METHOD

Supplement to Any Bass Method

T0052775

INTRODUCTION

Welcome to *Even More Easy Pop Bass Lines*, a collection of 20 pop and rock favorites arranged for easy bass. If you're an intermediate-level bassist, you've come to the right place; these well-known songs will have you playing, reading, and enjoying music in no time!

This book can be used on its own or as a supplement to the *Hal Leonard Bass Method* or any other intermediate-level bass method. The songs are arranged in order of difficulty. Each bass line is presented in an easy-to-read format—including lyrics to help you follow along and chords for optional accompaniment (by your teacher, if you have one).

ISBN 978-0-634-07355-7

HAL•LEONARD®
CORPORATION
7777 W. BLUEMOUND RD. P.O. BOX 13819 MILWAUKEE, WI 53213

Visit Hal Leonard Online at
www.halleonard.com

SONG STRUCTURE

The songs in this book have different sections, which may or may not include the following:

Intro
This is usually a short instrumental section that "introduces" the song at the beginning.

Verse
This is one of the main sections of a song and conveys most of the storyline. A song usually has several verses, all with the same music but each with different lyrics.

Chorus
This is often the most memorable section of a song. Unlike the verse, the chorus usually has the same lyrics every time it repeats.

Bridge
This section is a break from the rest of the song, often having a very different chord progression and feel.

Solo
This is an instrumental section, often played over the verse or chorus structure.

Outro
Similar to an intro, this section brings the song to an end.

ENDINGS & REPEATS

Many of the songs have some new symbols that you must understand before playing. Each of these represents a different type of ending.

1st and 2nd Endings
These are indicated by brackets and numbers. The first time through a song section, play the first ending and then repeat. The second time through, skip the first ending, and play through the second ending.

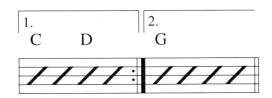

D.S.
This means "Dal Segno" or "from the sign." When you see this abbreviation above the staff, find the sign (𝄋) earlier in the song and resume playing from that point.

al Coda
This means "to the Coda," a concluding section in the song. If you see the words "D.S. al Coda," return to the sign (𝄋) earlier in the song and play until you see the words "To Coda," then skip to the Coda at the end of the song, indicated by the symbol: ⊕.

al Fine
This means "to the end." If you see the words "D.S. al Fine," return to the sign (𝄋) earlier in the song and play until you see the word "Fine."

D.C.
This means "Da Capo" or "from the head." When you see this abbreviation above the staff, return to the beginning (or "head") of the song and resume playing.

CONTENTS

EIGHT DAYS A WEEK

Words and Music by
JOHN LENNON and PAUL McCARTNEY

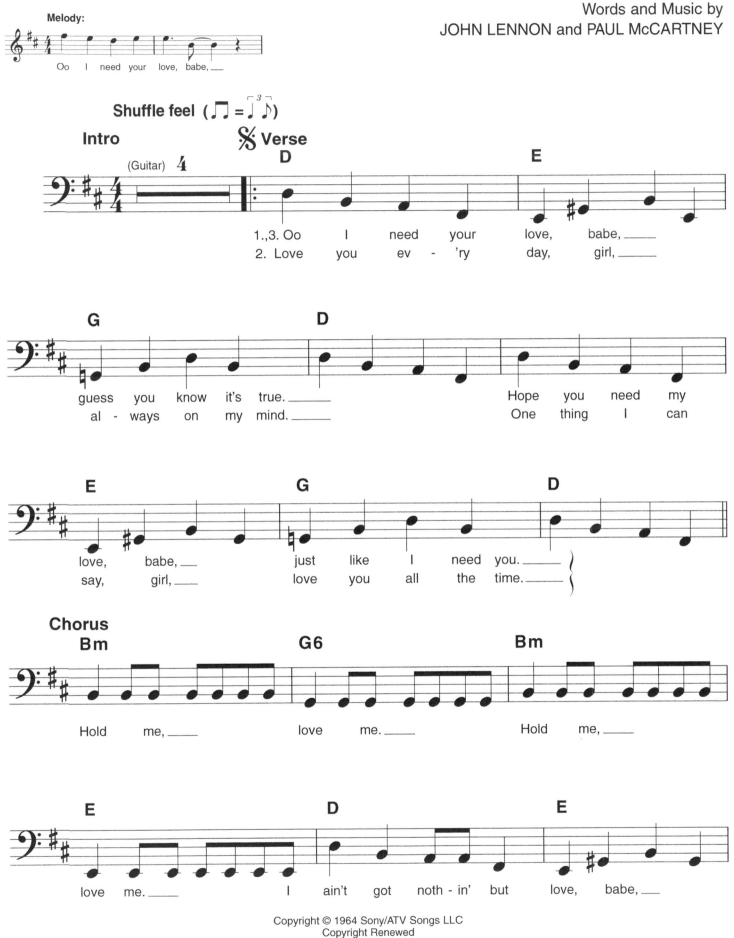

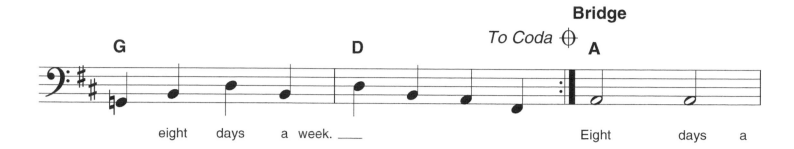

eight days a week. ____ Eight days a

week, I love _____ you. Eight days a

week is not e - nough to show I care. ____

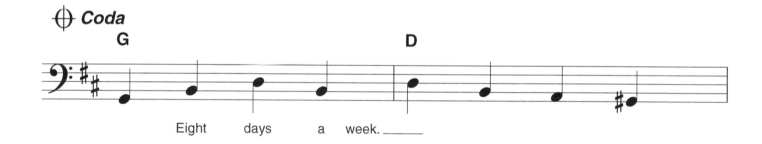

Eight days a week. ____

Eight days a week. ____

All Shook Up

Words and Music by
OTIS BLACKWELL and ELVIS PRESLEY

Melody:

A well a, bless my soul.___ What's...

Intro
Shuffle feel
G

Verse
G

1. A well a, bless my soul. ___ What's wrong with me? ___ I'm

itch - ing like a man ___ on a fuz - zy tree. ___ My friends say I'm act - ing

weird as a bug. ___ I'm in love! I'm all shook up! ___ Ooh, _____

ooh, ____   yeah, ____ yeah, _____ yeah. ____

Bridge

Well,   please   don't   ask   what's ____ on   my mind, ____ I'm a
tongue   gets   tired   when   I   try   to speak, ____ my ____

lit - tle   mixed   up   but   I'm   feel -   in'   fine. ____   When
in - sides   shake   like   a   leaf   on   a   tree. ____   There's

I'm   near   the   girl ____ that   I   love best, ____ my   heart   beats   so   it
on - ly   one   cure ____ for this   bod - y   of   mine, ____ that's   to   have   the   girl   that   I

Verse

scares   me   to   death!   2., 3. She   touched   my   hand   what   a   chill   I   got, ____ her
love   so   fine!

7

kiss - es are like ___ a vol - can - o that's hot. ___ I'm proud to say she's my

but - ter - cup. ___ I'm in love! I'm all shook up! ___ Ooh, _____

C   **D**   **G**

1.

___ ooh, ___ yeah, ___ yeah, _____ yeah. ___ My

2. **G**   **C**

___ yeah, _____ yeah; ___ ooh, _____ ooh, ___

D   **G**

___ yeah, ___ yeah, ___ I'm all shook up!

Radar Love

Words and Music by
GEORGE KOOYMANS and BARRY HAY

she sends a ca - ble com - ing in _____ from a - bove._
she sends a com - fort com - ing in _____ from a - bove._

_____ Don't need a phone at all. _____
_____ We don't need no let - ter at all. _____

Chorus

1. We've got a thing, ___ and that's a called ra - dar love._
2. We've got a thing, ___ that's called ra - dar love._

_____ We've got a wave _____ in the air. _____
_____ We've got a light _____ in the sky. _

Interlude

Ra - dar love. _____

2. The Ra - dar

Interlude

Play 32 times

love. ___
(Sing 1st time only)

11

Breakdown

N.C.

(Drums) 8

Play 4 times

E5

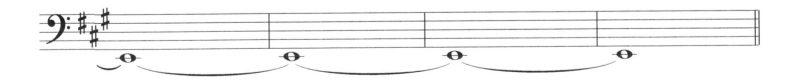

Outro

F♯m7

Play 4 times

INTO THE GREAT WIDE OPEN

Words and Music by
JEFF LYNNE and TOM PETTY

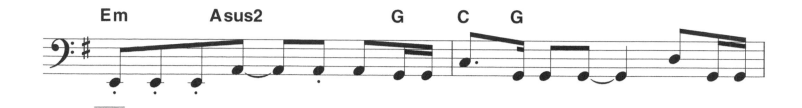

Interlude

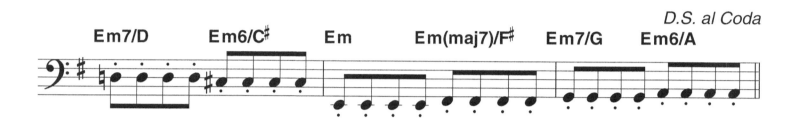

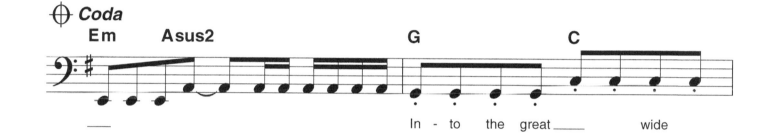

D.S. al Coda

Coda

In - to   the   great ___   wide

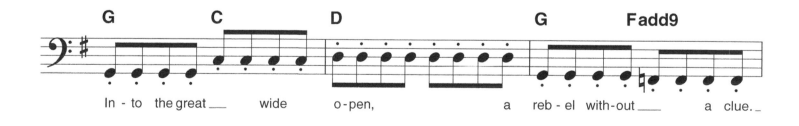

o - pen,   un - der them skies ___   of   blue.

In - to   the great ___   wide   o - pen,   a   reb - el   with-out ___   a   clue. _

Em   Asus2   G   C   G   C   G

Hey!

Blueberry Hill

Words and Music by AL LEWIS,
LARRY STOCK and VINCENT ROSE

and lin - gered un - til, _____ my dreams ___ came ___

true. _____ 1. The wind in the wil - low played _____

___ love's sweet mel - o - dy. _____ But all of those vows you made _____

___ were nev - er to be. _____ Tho' we're a - part ___

Chorus

_____ you're part of me still _____

___ for you were my thrill _____ on Blue - ber - ry

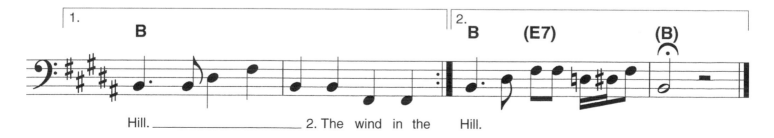

Hill. _____ 2. The wind in the Hill.

17

MAINSTREET

Words and Music by
BOB SEGER

THE JOKER

Words and Music by
STEVE MILLER, EDDIE CURTIS and AHMET ERTEGUN

say I'm do-in' you wrong, do-in' you wrong._____
real-ly love__your peach - es, wan-na shake your tree._____

But don't you wor-ry ba - by, don't wor-ry._____
Lov-ey dov-ey, lov-ey dov-ey, lov-ey dov-ey all the time;_____

'Cause I'm

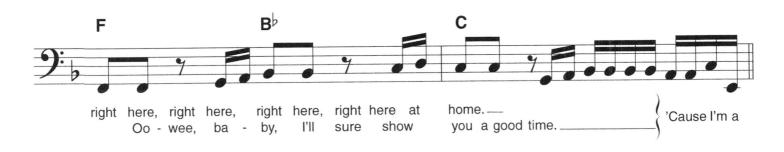

right here, right here, right here, right here at home.__
Oo-wee, ba - by, I'll sure show you a good time._____

'Cause I'm a

Chorus

pick - er, I'm a grin-ner, I'm a lov-er, and I'm a sin-ner.

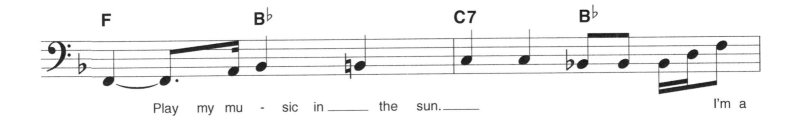

Play my mu - sic in _____ the sun._____

I'm a

jok-er, I'm a smok-er, I'm a mid-night__tok - er.

I get my lov-in' on ___ the run. ___
I sure don't want to hurt ___ no one. ___ Woo. ___

Guitar Solo

Woo. ___

2nd time, Fade out

ANOTHER ONE BITES THE DUST

Words and Music by
JOHN DEACON

Melody:

Steve walks war - i - ly down ___ the street,...

Intro

Verse

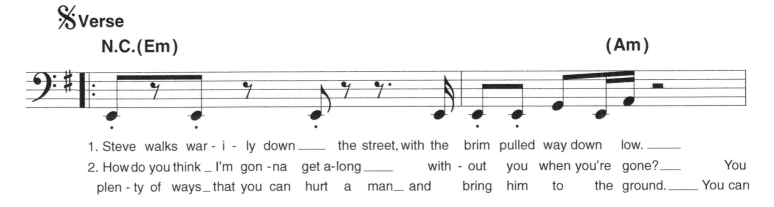

Ooh, let's go!

1. Steve walks war - i - ly down ___ the street, with the brim pulled way down low. ___
2. How do you think ___ I'm gon - na get a - long ___ with - out you when you're gone? ___ You

plen - ty of ways ___ that you can hurt a man ___ and bring him to the ground. ___ You can

CHEAP SUNGLASSES

Words and Music by
BILL F GIBBONS, DUSTY HILL and FRANK BEARD

Melody:

When you wake up in the morn - in'...

Intro
Rock Shuffle

1. When you

3. Now

Verse

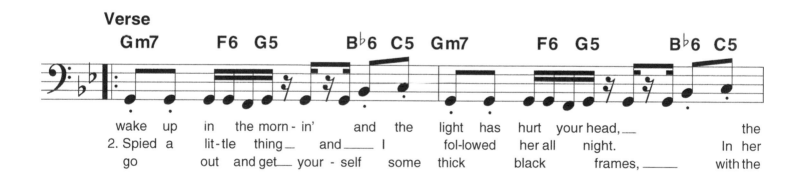

wake up in the morn - in' and the light has hurt your head, ___ the
2. Spied a lit - tle thing ___ and ___ I fol-lowed her all night. In her
go out and get ___ your - self some thick black frames, ___ with the

first thing you do _____ when you get up out of bed ___ is
funk - y fine Le - vi's ___ and her sweat-er kind a tight. ___ She had a
glass ___ so dark ___ they won't e - ven know your name. ___ And the

Guitar Solo
Cm7

B♭

Cm7

Dm7   **D**

Interlude
G5   **F6**   **G5**   **B♭6 C5 B♭6**   **G5**   **F6**   **G5**   **B♭6 C5 B♭6**

G5   **F6**   **G5**   **B♭6 C5 B♭6**   **G5**   **F6**   **G5**   *D.C. al Coda*

⊕ *Coda*
Outro
G5   *Repeat and fade*

STIR IT UP

Words and Music by
BOB MARLEY

ABC

Words and Music by ALPHONSO MIZELL,
FREDERICK PERREN, DEKE RICHARDS and BERRY GORDY

Chorus

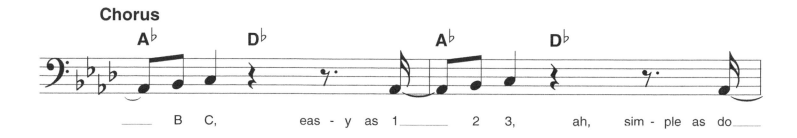

B C, eas - y as 1 2 3, ah, sim - ple as do

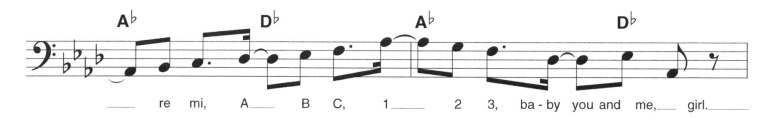

re mi, A B C, 1 2 3, ba - by you and me, girl.

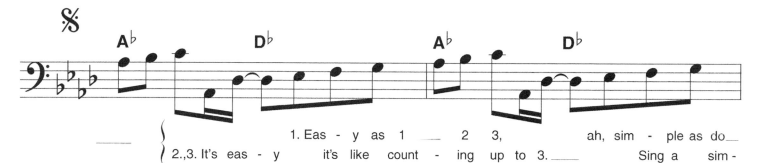

1. Eas - y as 1 2 3, ah, sim - ple as do
2.,3. It's eas - y it's like count - ing up to 3. Sing a sim -

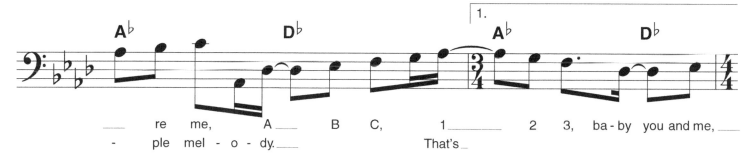

re me, A B C, 1 2 3, ba - by you and me,
- ple mel - o - dy. That's

girl. I'm

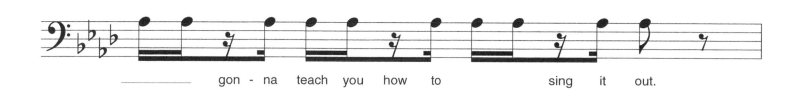

gon - na teach you how to sing it out.

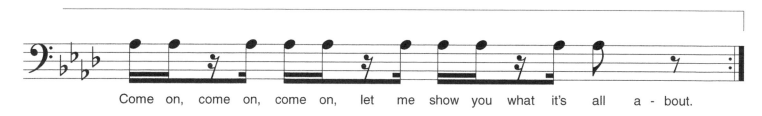

Come on, come on, come on, let me show you what it's all a - bout.

33

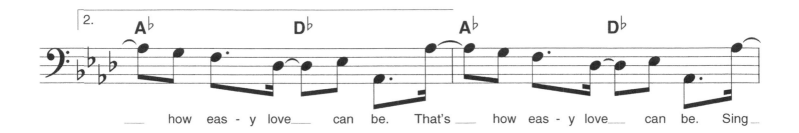

2.

how eas - y love ___ can be. That's ___ how eas - y love ___ can be. Sing

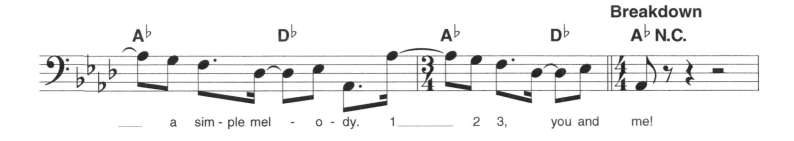

Breakdown

___ a sim - ple mel - o - dy. 1 ___ 2 3, you and me!

(Drums)

Shake it, shake it ba - by. Come on, now

shake it, shake it ba - by. Oo, ___ oo. Shake it, shake it ba - by. Ho!

1 2 3, ba - by. Oo, ___ oo. A B C, ba - by. Now, ___ now.

D.S. and fade

Do re mi, ba - by. Now! That's ___ how eas - y love ___ can be.

UNDER PRESSURE

Words and Music by
FREDDIE MERCURY, JOHN DEACON,
BRIAN MAY, ROGER TAYLOR and DAVID BOWIE

care for___ the peo - ple on the edge of___ the

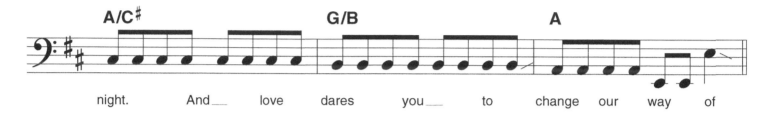

night. And___ love dares you___ to change our way of

Chorus

car - ing___ a - bout our - selves. This is___ our

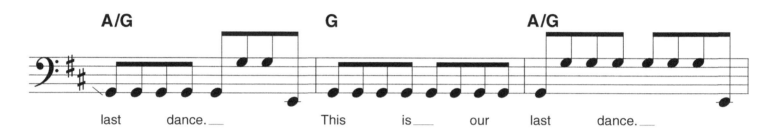

last dance.___ This is___ our last dance.___

Outro

This is___ our - selves. Un - der pres-sure,

un-der pres-sure,

pres-sure.

COME TOGETHER

Words and Music by
JOHN LENNON and PAUL McCARTNEY

A5

hair   down   to   his   knee._____
"I   know you,_____   you   know   me."
feet   down   be - low_____   his   knee._____
"One and one _____   and   one_____   is   three."_____

1.
G5

Got   to   be   a   jok - er   he   just   do   what   he   please. ____

2.
G5

One   thing   I   can   tell   you   is   you   got   to   be   free. _____
Hold   you   in   his   arm - chair,   you   can   feel   his   dis - ease. _____   } Come to - geth -
Got   to   be   good   look - ing   'cause   he   so   hard   to   see. _____

Chorus   *To Coda 1*
B5   **A5**   **G5**   **A5**   **Dm7**

- er   right   now, ___   o - ver me. ___

To Coda 2   *D.S. al Coda 1*
                                                        (take 2nd ending)

Shoot   me,   shoot   me,   shoot   me.

Coda 1   **Keyboard Solo**
Dm7   **D5**

___   Shoot   me.   Right. ___

Come.

Guitar Solo
A5

D.S. al Coda 2
(take 2nd ending)

Dm7

Coda 2

Outro
D5

Shoot   me.   Oh.

Play 10 times and fade

D5

Come to-geth - er,   yeah.

One Thing Leads to Another

Words and Music by
CY CURNIN, JAMIE WEST-ORAM, ADAM WOODS,
RUPERT GREENALL and ALFRED AGIUS

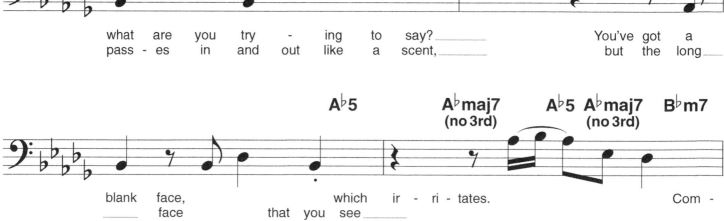

mu - ni - cate, pull out your par - ty piece.
comes from liv - ing close to your fears._____

You see di -
If this is

A♭5   **A♭maj7 (no 3rd)**   **A♭5**   **A♭maj7 (no 3rd)**   **B♭m7**

men - sions   in   two,_____
up,   then I'm up,   but you're run - ning out of sight.

state your case with black or white._____
You've seen your name on the walls.

But when one____
And when one____

A♭5   **A♭maj7 (no 3rd)**   **A♭5**   **A♭maj7 (no 3rd)**   **B♭m7**

____ lit - tle cross leads to shots, grit your teeth.
____ lit - tle bump leads to shock, miss a beat.

You run for cov - er so dis - creet.
You run for cov - er, and there's heat.

Why don't____ they do____

Chorus

B♭m7   **A♭5**   **A♭maj7 (no 3rd)**   **A♭5**   **A♭maj7 (no 3rd)**   **B♭m7**

____ what they say?   Say____ what you mean. Oh ba - by,

A♭5

one thing leads to an-oth - er. You told me some-thing wrong. I know I lis-ten too long.

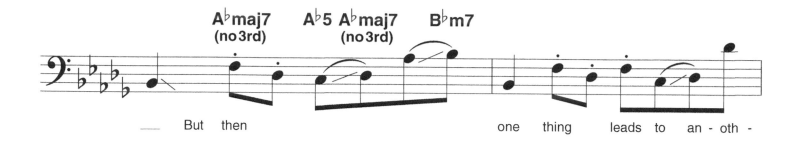

A♭maj7 (no 3rd) A♭5 A♭maj7 (no 3rd) B♭m7

____ But then   one thing leads to an - oth -

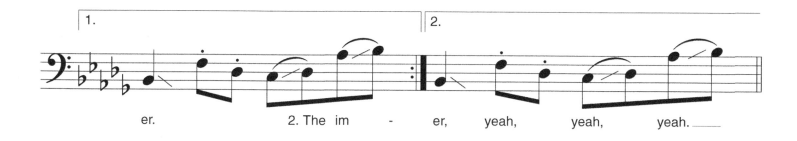

1.   2.

er.   2. The im -   er,   yeah,   yeah,   yeah. ____

Outro

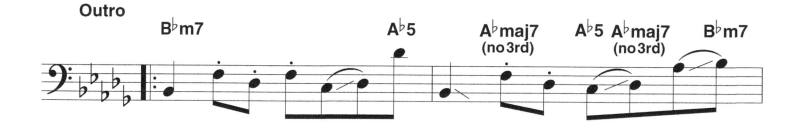

B♭m7   A♭5 A♭maj7 (no 3rd) A♭5 A♭maj7 (no 3rd) B♭m7

Repeat and fade

IRON MAN

Words and Music by
FRANK IOMMI, JOHN OSBOURNE,
WILLIAM WARD and TERENCE BUTLER

Interlude

To Coda ⊕

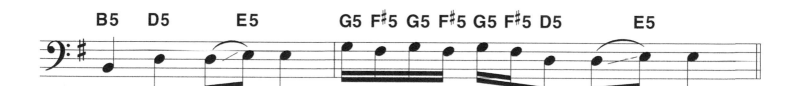

Verse

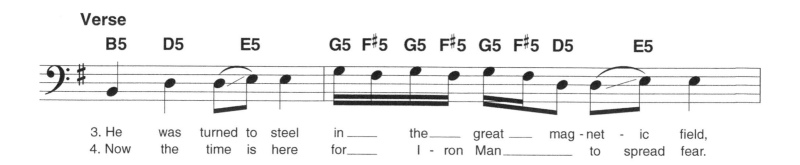

3. He was turned to steel in ____ the ____ great ____ mag-net - ic field,
4. Now the time is here for____ I - ron Man____ to spread fear.

Guitar Solo

B5

D5   **E5**   **G5 F♯5 G5 F♯5 G5 F♯5 D5**   **E5**

D.S. al Coda
(take 2nd ending)

B5   **D5**   **E5**   **G5 F♯5 G5 F♯5 G5 F♯5 D5**   **E5**

⊕ *Coda*
(A5)   **Double time**   **(Em)**

Play 8 times   **N.C.(E5)**

(D5)   **(C♯5)**

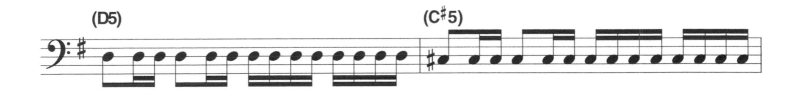

Outro

SWEET EMOTION

Words and Music by
STEVEN TYLER and TOM HAMILTON

Melody:

Talk a-bout things and no - bod - y cares,

Intro

Play 7 times

Chorus

N.C.(A)

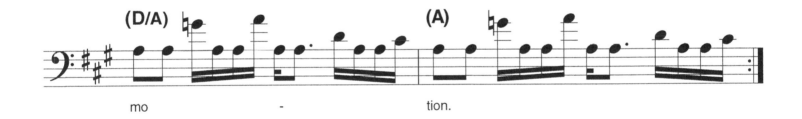

Sweet _____ e -

(D/A)   (A)

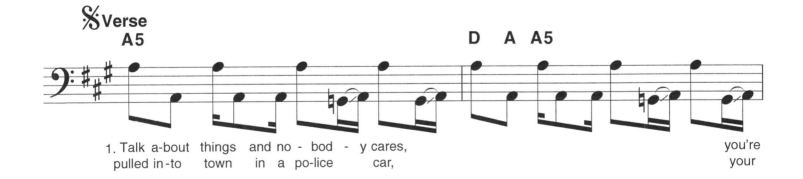

mo - tion.

𝄋 Verse
A5

D   A   A5

1. Talk a-bout things and no - bod - y cares,
   pulled in-to town in a po-lice car,

you're
your

wear-in' out things that no-bod-y wears.
dad-dy said I took you just a lit-tle too far.
You're
You're

call-in' my name, but I got-ta make clear,
tell-in' her things but your girl-friend lied,
I
you

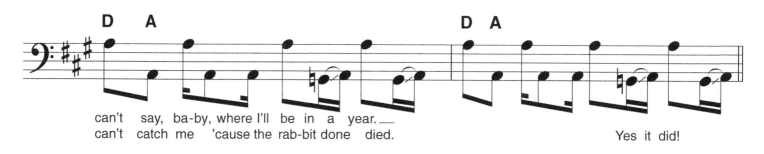

can't say, ba-by, where I'll be in a year. __
can't catch me 'cause the rab-bit done died.
Yes it did!

Interlude
N.C.

2. Some
4. You

Verse

sweet-talk-in' ma-ma with a face like a gent
stand in the front just a shak-in' yo ass,
said my
I'll

get up and go _____ must-'ve got up and went. _____
take you back - stage ____ you can drink from my glass.

Well, I got good news, she's a real ___ good li - ar,
I'm talk-in' 'bout some -thin' you can sure un - der - stand,

'cause my back - stage boo - gie set yo' pants on fire.
'cause a month on the road and I'll be eat - in' from your hand.

Interlude
N.C.

To Coda ⊕

Chorus
N.C.(A)

Sweet _____

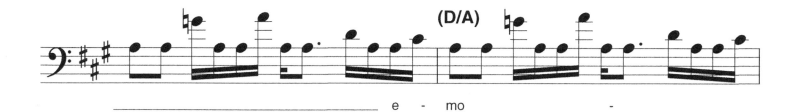

(D/A)

_____ e - mo -

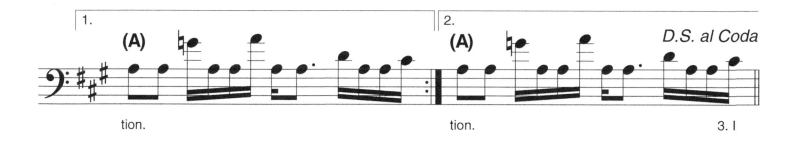

|1.
(A)

|2.
(A)

D.S. al Coda

tion.   tion.   3. I

⊕ *Coda*

Outro
N.C.(E7)

Play 12 times and fade

I WISH

Words and Music by
STEVIE WONDER

Look - ing back on when I____

Intro
Funk

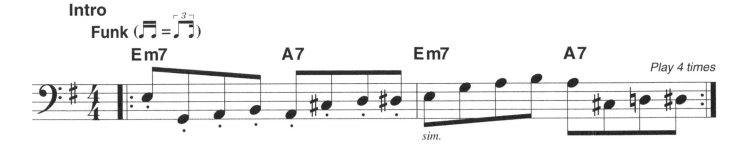

%. Verse

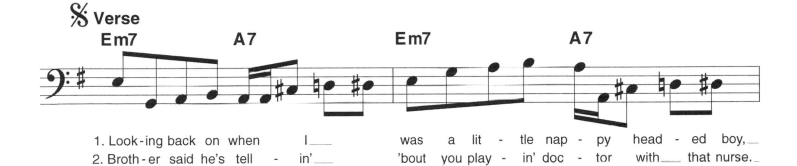

1. Look-ing back on when I____ was a lit - tle nap - py head - ed boy,
2. Broth - er said he's tell - in'____ 'bout you play - in' doc - tor with____ that nurse.

then my on - ly wor - ry____ was for Christ-mas what would be__ my toy.
Just don't tell and I'll give you____ an - y - thing__ you want_in this whole wide_

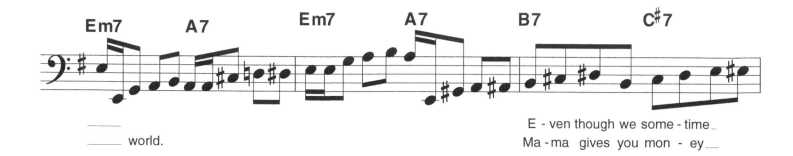

E - ven though we some - time___
Ma - ma gives you mon - ey___

_____
_____ world.

would not get a thing,___
for Sun - day school,___

we were hap - py with the___
you trade just for can - dy___

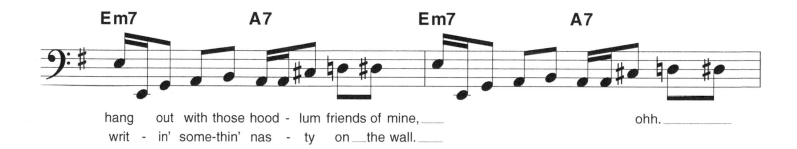

joy the day__ would bring. ___
af - ter church__ is through.__

Sneak - in' out___ the back___ door,___ to
Smok - in' cig - a-rettes___ and __

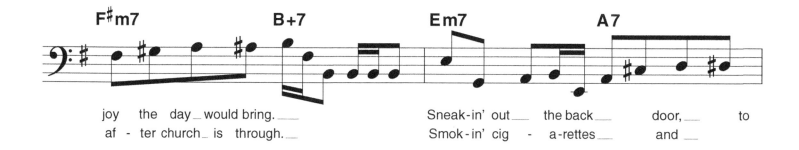

hang out with those hood - lum friends of mine,___
writ - in' some-thin' nas - ty on __the wall.___

ohh. _____

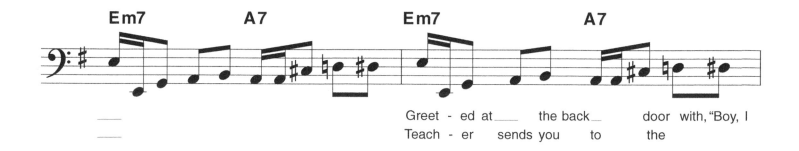

___
___

Greet - ed at___ the back___ door with, "Boy, I
Teach - er sends you to the

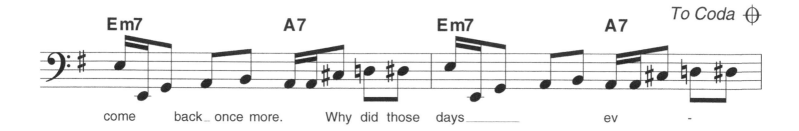

come   back— once more.   Why did those   days_____   ev   -

er   have— to   go?   'Cause I   loved them   so_____

D.S. al Coda

⊕ **Coda**

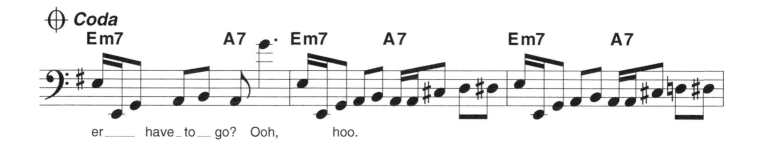

er_____   have— to— go?   Ooh,   hoo.

Outro

Repeat and fade

BADGE

Words and Music by
ERIC CLAPTON and GEORGE HARRISON

Melody:

Think-in' 'bout the times you drove___ in my car.___

Intro

Verse

1. Think-in' 'bout the   times   you drove___ in my car.___
2. I told you not to   wan - der 'round___ in the dark.___

Think-in' that I
I told you 'bout the

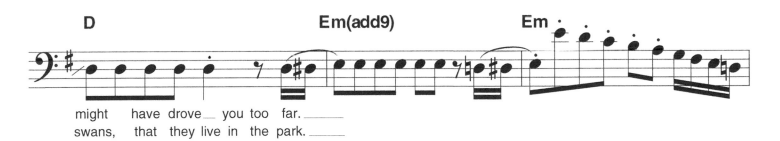

might   have drove___ you too   far.___
swans,   that they live in the park.___

And I'm think-in' 'bout the   love   that you laid on my ta - ble.
Then I told you 'bout our   kid,   now he's mar-ried to Ma - ble.

Verse

3. Talk - in' 'bout a girl that looks___ quite like you.

She did - n't have the time to wait ___ in the queue. ___

She cried a - way her

life since she fell off the cra - dle.

BRICK HOUSE

Words and Music by LIONEL RICHIE,
RONALD LaPREAD, WALTER ORANGE, MILAN WILLIAMS,
THOMAS McCLARY and WILLIAM KING

Melody:

Ow, she's a brick house. _____

Intro
N.C.

Uh, _____ uh, ___ uh. ___

*P = Pop

Uh.

Woo,   wee!

Chorus

Ow, she's a brick   house. ___

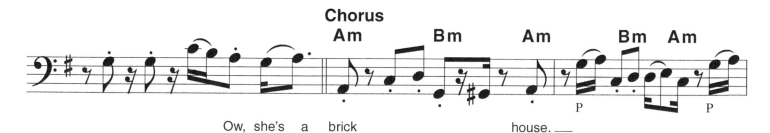

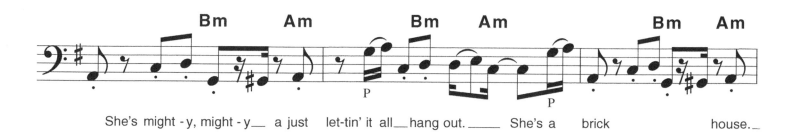

She's might-y, might-y___ a just let-tin' it all___hang out. ___ She's a brick   house.___

Bm   Am   Bm   Am

___ I like lad-ies stacked__and that's a fact.__

Bm   Am   Bm   Am

Ain't hold-in' noth-in' back.__Ow, she's a brick house.__

Bm   Am   Bm   Am

___ Well, we're to-geth - er ev-'ry-bod - y knows, ___

Verse

Bm   Am   Am7

this is how the sto - ry goes. ___

1. She knows she's got ev - 'ry-thing.__
2. The clothes she wear, ___ her

___ That a wom-an needs to get a man. Well, well.
sex-y ways ___ make an old __ man __ wish for young-er days__yeah, __ yeah.

How can she lose,__with the stuff she use? Thir-ty-six, twen-ty-four, __ thir-ty-six.
She _ knows she's built and knows how to please. __ Sure 'nough can knock a strong __

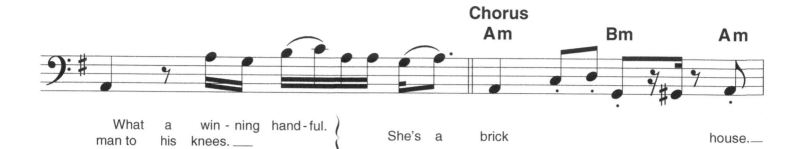

Chorus

What a win-ning hand-ful.
man to his knees. ___ She's a brick house. ___

She's might - y, might - y, ___ just

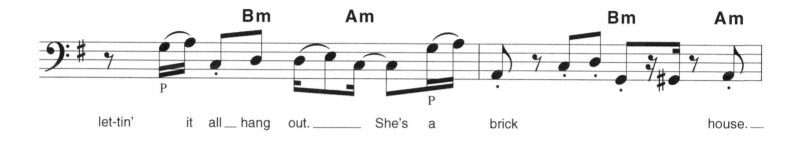

let-tin' it all ___ hang out. ___ She's a brick house. ___

Oh, I like la - dies stacked and that's a fact.

Ain't hold-in' noth-in' back. Ow, she's a brick ___ house. ___

Well, ___ she's the one, ___ the on - ly one ___

64

she's the one,__ the on - ly one ____ built like an Am - a - zon. __

Bridge

Shake it down, shake it down, shake it now now. __Shake it down, shake it down, shake it, now, now. __

Shake it down, shake it down, shake it, now, now. __Shake it down, shake it down, shake it, shake it.

Interlude

____ Shake it down, shake it down, shake it. Oh, a

Outro

brick house.____

I wan-na brick house. ____

HIGHER GROUND

Words and Music by
STEVIE WONDER

Melody:

Peo - ple, _____

Intro
Triplet feel

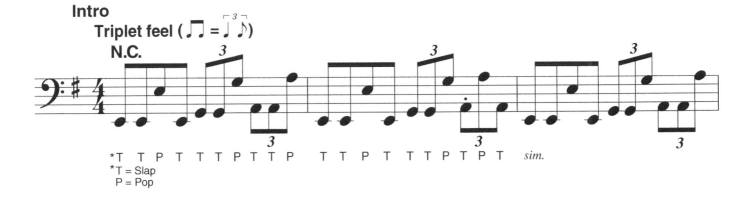

*T = Slap
P = Pop

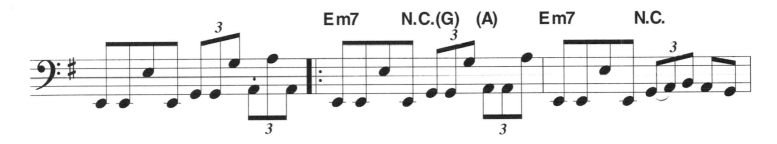

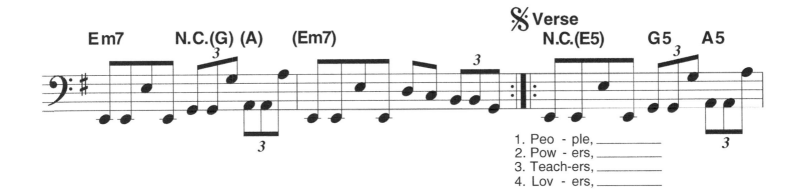

1. Peo - ple, _____
2. Pow - ers, _____
3. Teach-ers, _____
4. Lov - ers, _____

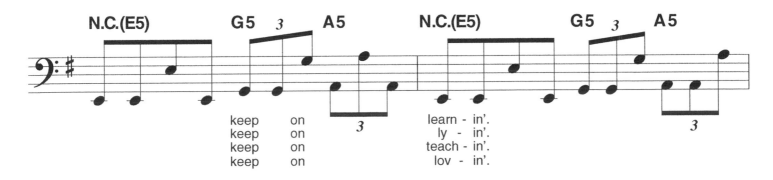

keep on learn - in'.
keep on ly - in'.
keep on teach - in'.
keep on lov - in'.

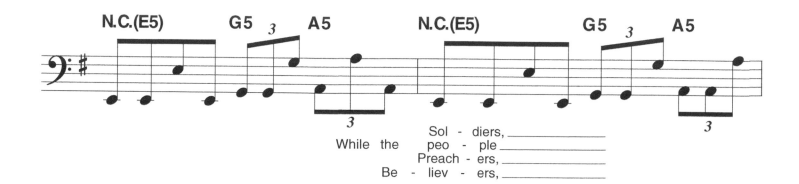

Sol - diers, _____
While the peo - ple _____
Preach - ers, _____
Be - liev - ers, _____

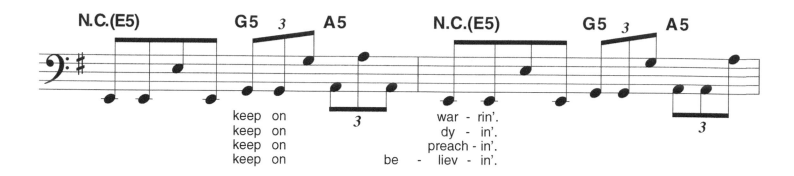

keep on   war - rin'.
keep on   dy - in'.
keep on   preach - in'.
keep on   be - liev - in'.

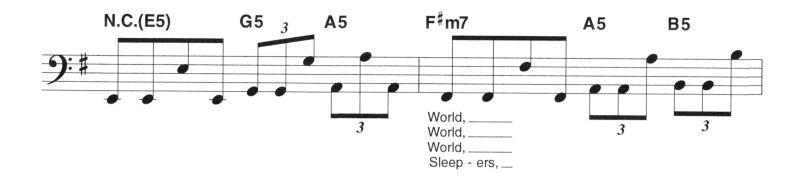

World, _____
World, _____
World, _____
Sleep - ers, __

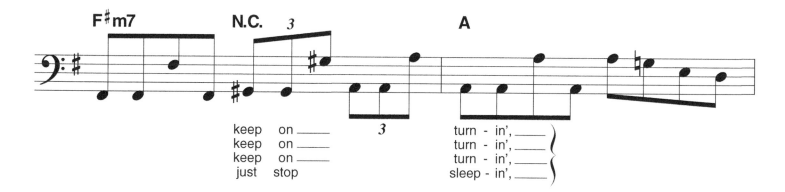

keep   on _____   turn - in', _____
keep   on _____   turn - in', _____
keep   on _____   turn - in', _____
just   stop   sleep - in', _____

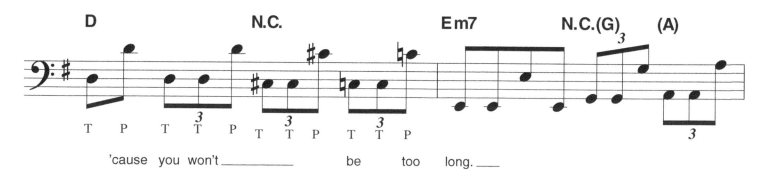

'cause you won't _____   be   too   long. ___

68

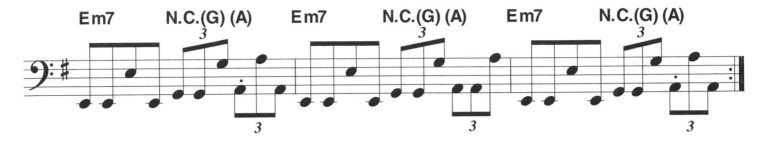

Chorus

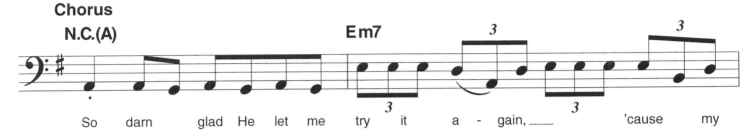

So darn glad He let me try it a - gain, ____ 'cause my

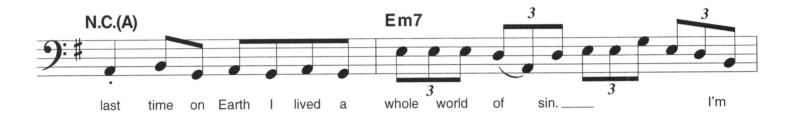

last time on Earth I lived a whole world of sin. ____ I'm

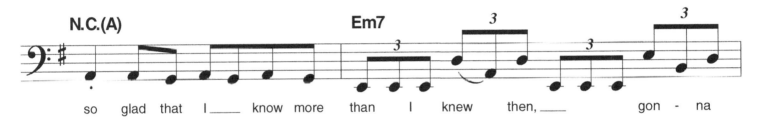

so glad that I ____ know more than I knew then, ____ gon - na

2nd time, to Coda ⊕

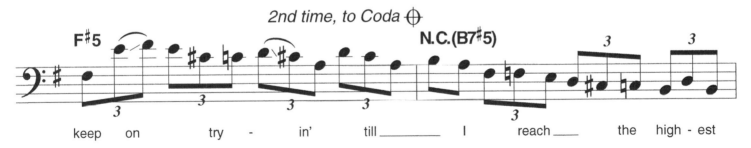

keep on try - in' till _____ I reach ____ the high - est

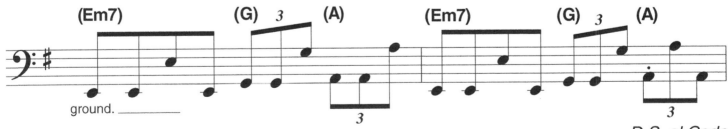

ground. _____

D.S. al Coda
(take repeat)

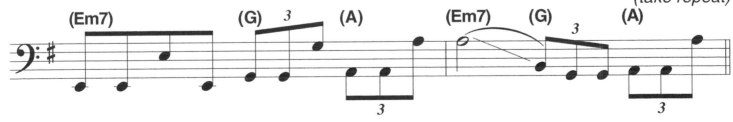

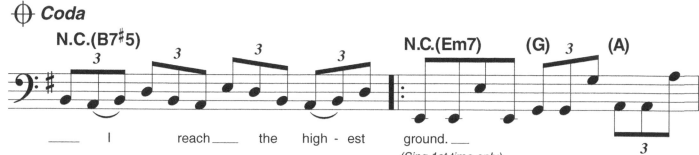

Coda

N.C.(B7♯5)   N.C.(Em7)   (G)   (A)

____ I   reach____ the   high - est   ground. ____

(Sing 1st time only)

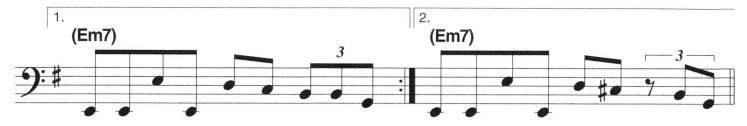

(Em7)   (G)   (A)

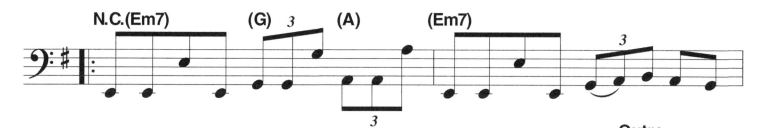

1. (Em7)   2. (Em7)

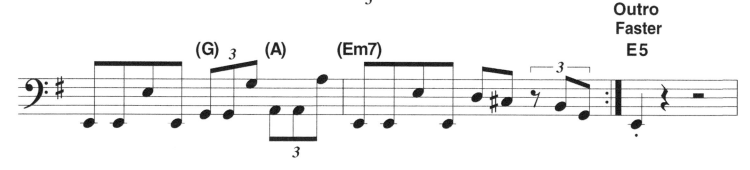

N.C.(Em7)   (G)   (A)   (Em7)

(G)   (A)   (Em7)   **Outro**
                                         Faster
                                         E 5

(Guitar)   E 5   G 5   A 5   G 5

E 5   G 5   A 5   G 5   E 5

HAL LEONARD
BASS METHOD

METHOD BOOKS

by Ed Friedland

BOOK 1
Book 1 teaches: tuning; playing position; musical symbols; notes within the first five frets; common bass lines, patterns and rhythms; rhythms through eighth notes; playing tips and techniques; more than 100 great songs, riffs and examples; and more! The audio includes 44 full-band tracks for demonstration or play-along.
00695067 Book Only.................................. $7.99
00695068 Book/Online Audio.................. $12.99

BOOK 2
Book 2 continues where Book 1 left off and teaches: the box shape; moveable boxes; notes in fifth position; major and minor scales; the classic blues line; the shuffle rhythm; tablature; and more!
00695069 Book Only.................................. $7.99
00695070 Book/Online Audio.................. $12.99

BOOK 3
With the third book, progressing students will learn more great songs, riffs and examples; sixteenth notes; playing off chord symbols; slap and pop techniques; hammer-ons and pull-offs; playing different styles and grooves; and more.
00695071 Book Only.................................. $7.99
00695072 Book/Online Audio.................. $12.99

COMPOSITE
This money-saving edition contains Books 1, 2 and 3.
00695073 Book Only................................ $17.99
00695074 Book/Online Audio.................. $24.99

DVD
Play your favorite songs in no time with this DVD! Covers: tuning, notes in first through third position, rhythms through eighth notes, fingerstyle and pick playing, 4/4 and 3/4 time, and more! Includes 6 full songs and on-screen music notation. 68 minutes.
00695849 DVD $19.95

BASS FOR KIDS
by Chad Johnson
Bass for Kids is a fun, easy course that teaches children to play bass guitar faster than ever before. Popular songs such as "Crazy Train," "Every Breath You Take," "A Hard Day's Night" and "Wild Thing" keep kids motivated, and the clean, simple page layouts ensure their attention remains focused on one concept at a time.
00696449 Book/Online Audio $12.99

REFERENCE BOOKS

BASS SCALE FINDER
by Chad Johnson
Learn to use the entire fretboard with the *Bass Scale Finder*. This book contains over 1,300 scale diagrams for the most important 17 scale types.
00695781 6" x 9" Edition....................... $7.99
00695778 9" x 12" Edition..................... $7.99

BASS ARPEGGIO FINDER
by Chad Johnson
This extensive reference guide lays out over 1,300 arpeggio shapes. 28 different qualities are covered for each key, and each quality is presented in four different shapes.
00695817 6" x 9" Edition....................... $7.99
00695816 9" x 12" Edition..................... $7.99

MUSIC THEORY FOR BASSISTS
by Sean Malone
Acclaimed bassist and composer Sean Malone will explain the written language of music, using easy-to-understand terms and concepts, diagrams, and much more. The audio provides 96 tracks of examples, demonstrations, and play-alongs.
00695756 Book/Online Audio $17.99

STYLE BOOKS

BASS LICKS
by Ed Friedland
This comprehensive supplement to any bass method will help students learn over 200 great bass licks, lines and grooves in many rhythmic styles. *Bass Licks* illustrates how simple melodic patterns can become the springboard for group improvisation or the foundation of a song.
00696035 Book/Online Audio $14.99

BASS LINES
by Matt Scharfglass
500 expertly written bass lines, riffs and fills in a wide variety of musical genres are included in this comprehensive collection to help players expand their bass vocabulary. The examples cover many tempos, keys and feels, and include easy bass lines for beginners on up to advanced riffs for more experienced bassists.
00148194 Book/Online Audio $19.99

BLUES BASS
by Ed Friedland
Learn to play studying the songs of B.B. King, Stevie Ray Vaughan, Muddy Waters, Albert King, the Allman Brothers, T-Bone Walker, and many more. Learn riffs from blues classics including: Born Under a Bad Sign • Hideaway • Hoochie Coochie Man • Killing Floor • Pride and Joy • Sweet Home Chicago • The Thrill Is Gone • and more.
00695870 Book/Online Audio $14.99

COUNTRY BASS
by Glenn Letsch
21 songs, including: Act Naturally • Boot Scootin' Boogie • Crazy • Honky Tonk Man • Love You Out Loud • Luckenbach, Texas (Back to the Basics of Love) • No One Else on Earth • Ring of Fire • Southern Nights • Streets of Bakersfield • Whose Bed Have Your Boots Been Under? • and more.
00695928 Book/Online Audio $17.99

FRETLESS BASS
by Chris Kringel
18 songs, including: Bad Love • Continuum • Even Flow • Everytime You Go Away • Hocus Pocus • I Could Die for You • Jelly Roll • King of Pain • Kiss of Life • Lady in Red • Tears in Heaven • Very Early • What I Am • White Room • more.
00695850... $19.99

FUNK BASS
by Chris Kringel
This is your complete guide to learning the basics of grooving and soloing funk bass. Songs include: Can't Stop • I'll Take You There • Let's Groove • Stay • What Is Hip • and more.
00695792 Book/Online Audio.............. $22.99

R&B BASS
by Glenn Letsch
This book/audio pack uses actual classic R&B, Motown, soul and funk songs to teach you how to groove in the style of James Jamerson, Bootsy Collins, Bob Babbitt, and many others. The 19 songs include: For Once in My Life • Knock on Wood • Mustang Sally • Respect • Soul Man • Stand by Me • and more.
00695823 Book/Online Audio $17.99

ROCK BASS
by Sean Malone
This book/audio pack uses songs from a myriad of rock genres to teach the key elements of rock bass. Includes: Another One Bites the Dust • Beast of Burden • Money • Roxanne • Smells like Teen Spirit • and more.
00695801 Book/Online Audio.............. $21.99

SUPPLEMENTARY SONGBOOKS

These great songbooks correlate with Books 1-3 of the *Hal Leonard Bass Method*, giving students great songs to play while they're still learning! The audio tracks include great accompaniment and demo tracks.

EASY POP BASS LINES
20 great songs that students in Book 1 can master. Includes: Come as You Are • Crossfire • Great Balls of Fire • Imagine • Surfin' U.S.A. • Takin' Care of Business • Wild Thing • and more.
00695810 Book Only.............................. $9.99
00695809 Book/Online Audio.............. $15.99

MORE EASY POP BASS LINES
20 great songs for Level 2 students. Includes: Bad, Bad Leroy Brown • Crazy Train • I Heard It Through the Grapevine • My Generation • Pride and Joy • Ramblin' Man • Summer of '69 • and more.
00695819 Book Only............................ $12.99
00695818 Book/Online Audio.............. $16.99

EVEN MORE EASY POP BASS LINES
20 great songs for Level 3 students, including: ABC • Another One Bites the Dust • Brick House • Come Together • Higher Ground • Iron Man • The Joker • Sweet Emotion • Under Pressure • more.
00695821 Book $9.99
00695820 Book/Online Audio.............. $16.99

Visit Hal Leonard online at
www.halleonard.com